September 2016

Dedicated to my beautiful wife Carú

1. The Archipelago

And one day you wake up in the Seychelles...

In a nutshell, Seychelles is an archipelago of 115 Islands located in the Indian Ocean, off East Africa, known worldwide for the most beautiful beaches in the world, preserved coral reefs and natural reserves, awesome diving sites, rare wildlife preservation and for the slow paced, relaxing lifestyle called "creole spirit".

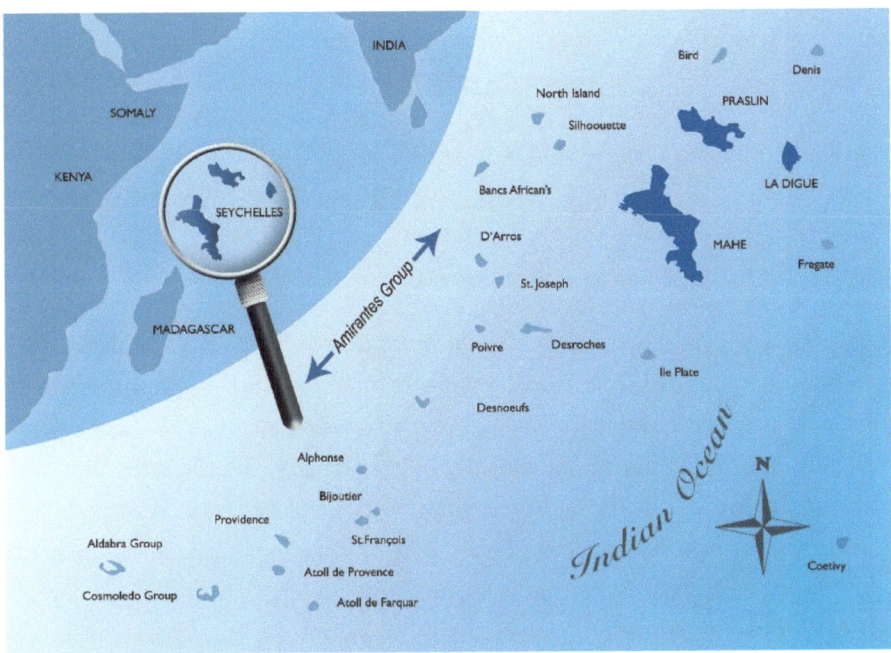

With a population of roughly 92.000 people and Victoria being the smallest capital city in the world, there is an airport in the main Island Mahé, offering international flights and connecting the second largest island, called Praslin with a quick 15 minute flight.

Praslin has around 8.000 inhabitants, home of the Vallée de Mai, which legend say it's the original "Garden of Eden", and Anse Lazio, a beach of extraordinary natural beauty, with coconut trees lying almost horizontally touching the utterly transparent waters, in addition to big granitic boulders carved by the ocean, emerging in the middle of the sea, to compose the absolutely most perfect idyllic scenario of a vacation of a lifetime.

Praslin is also gateway to La Digue; through a 15 minute catamaran jetty, you can reach the third largest inhabited island, which for local standards will be no more than 2.800 people. While in Mahé and Praslin there are several big hotels and resorts, La Digue accommodation is basically made up from small family run guest houses, with a special touch to hospitality, and self-catering properties, great for families or groups, if you want to feel home far from home.

Mahé, Praslin and La Digue are granitic Islands – contrasting with most of the other islands, which are coralline. The three islands have a contrasted relief, with big tops, high mountains and luxurious forests. This only means one thing: lots of up & downs, through narrow curvy roads, on all three islands.

It is known that the Seychelles have been discovered by the Portuguese navigator Vasco da Gama, on its way to the Indias; da Gama took note of the location of these Islands and then sailed away. He might have thought about lounging in the white crystal-like sands and beautiful scenery of one of the Islands for some time, but being concerned with commerce of spices, and Seychelles not being inhabited, it was a place of little interest for a man with such mission. The resorts and luxury island hotels were still to come, so he sailed away. Then came the French, and then the British, and centuries after, Seychelles became an independent Presidential Republic in 1976.

Although more than 2.000 km from the closest land, Seychelles is considered part of Africa and boosts the highest Human Development Index (HDI) and income per capita of the whole continent.

The country has a strong share of their GDP attached to Tourism, which is the main Industry employing great part of the population directly and indirectly and attracting numerous international hotel chains to this destination of turquoise beaches, white sands and great weather all year round.

Quite close to the line of Equator, sunrise is religiously all-year-round at about 6:30am and sunset, well, at 6:30pm. To be precise, Mahé is just 4 degrees south of the Equator. There is plenty of daylight to take advantage of all kind of sports and activities.

Temperature is stable throughout the year, ranging from 26 to 32 degrees Celsius. With a mountainous profile, every day there's rain in Mahé, normally short half hour showers. The rainy Season however is very rainy! Lasts from December to beginning of February – and sometimes it does rain the whole day in that Season.

The British have left their heritage in the country: the electricity is 220v, with the UK type of electrical plug and people drive on the left side of the roads, which will require some special attention for those not very used to that; people do park on the right side of the roads, anytime, for no special reason or just because the small local market they're going to is on the same right side of the road. Need to be alert to that as well.

2. Cycling in Seychelles

From my experience, there are only three islands where you can cycle and are Mahé, Praslin and La Digue.

You will not find single-tracks or gravel roads in any of the three islands, everything is paved. And well paved indeed – mostly asphalt but if you go deep in the mountains, even the narrowest back roads are cement paved, which makes these roads look a lot like cycling paths. With the difference that they're seldom flat; instead they're very steep, both going up and down.

Putting it very clear: the roads are narrow, curvy and normally steep. There are steep rain drains on both sides of the road, but the traffic is light, actually very well behaved compared to other places in the world. The public transportation buses are a bit noisy and smoky but I've always found the drivers very courteous with cyclists. However, people are still not used to see and share roads with cyclists, so to cycle in Seychelles it will require lots of attention.

As I'm used to explain to people that look surprised when I tell them that I normally cycle around Mahé, if you go out in early morning, and manage to get away from the Victoria-Airport-Anse Royal axis before the traffic starts to build-up, you'll find a completely different place to ride around.

Traffic past Anse Royal and going down South, is practically inexistent, especially in early weekend mornings. You will be able to relax and enjoy the ride, the scenery and landscape along the coastline and you'll see very few cars around indeed.

Same thing in the Island of Praslin, if you're around the North, far from the Airport-Jetty driveway, you're literally in paradise. Relax, enjoy the scenery. Take a deep breath and inhale the best quality of air in the planet, as it has been reported by the Environmental Performance Index 2016.

The neighboring Island La Digue is *hors concours*. It is made for bikes, and you can only go around in bike. People do everything on their bikes, accessorized with supermarket baskets on its rear wheels to carry all sorts of things. You'll really feel at home and the place is small, after about two hours around you'll basically have been everywhere in the Island, lots of fun.

3. The Rides

For the purpose of organizing this compilation, we will cover the rides in Mahé in depth, dividing it in 4 parts, and then highlighting a weekend ride to Praslin and extension to La Digue.

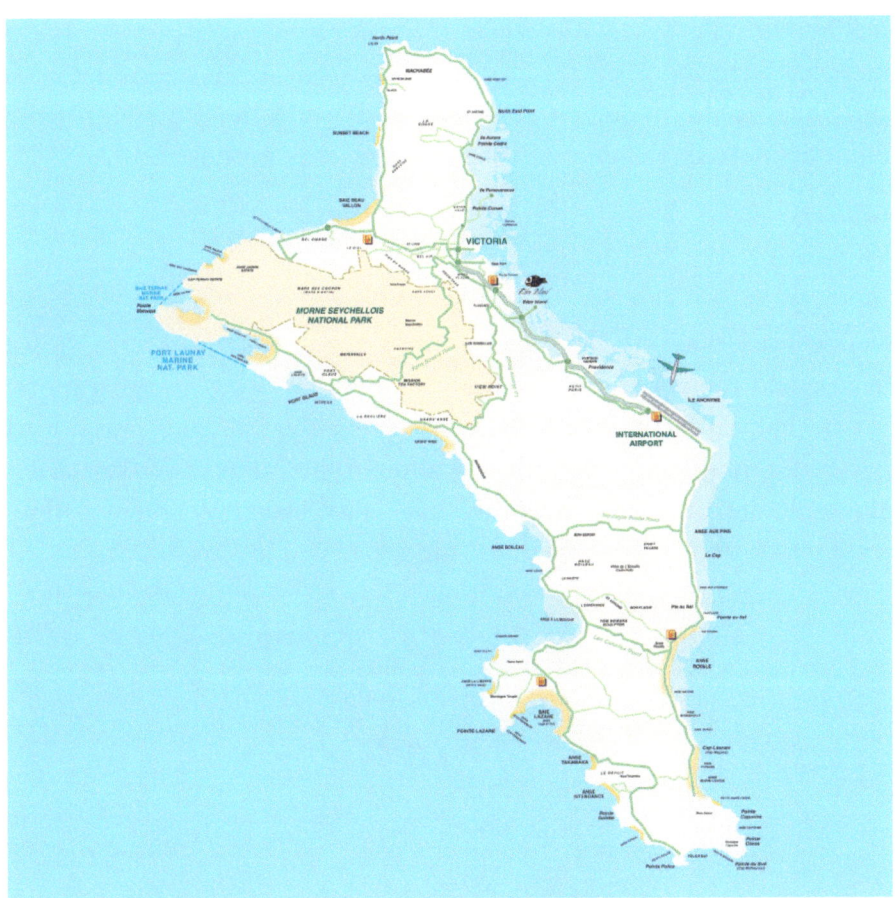

First **The North**, with Beau Vallon, Bel Ombre, Glacis, Vista del Mar, La Gogue Dam and La Retraite. And, of course, the tiniest capital of State in the world: Victoria.

The **Climbs**, Sans Souci and La Misère roads, that traverse the Island longitudinally from one side to the other and are the steepest climbs around.

The **South East**, with Anse aux Pins, Anse Royal and the three smaller climbs Montagne Posée, Les Canelles and Takamaka, also crossing from one side of the Island to the other.

Finally, the **West** side deserves a classification of its own. It's a gorgeous territory, a succession of beaches one after the other, with small hills in the middle, and this will last for around 25 Km, from South tip in Anse Takamaka to the north most point Port Launay.

3.1. North

We start our bike ride in Victoria, the Capital, in front of the Clock Tower, and then pass one of the only 3 semaphores in the country (wow!), to turn left to the St. Louis road up the hill. This is the road that connects the capital to Beau Vallon. Quite narrow for two lanes and with big guts at the borders, it's just like any other road in Seychelles, better to do early in the morning, with less traffic.

It will be 1200 m up-hill with moderate ascension to the peak; this is where closer to the bus station, right in front of the white walls of the Botanica Residence and Resort, you'll take the road on your left, where it says Chemin Le Niol road.

It's a 1500 m dead-end, which you can skip it if you don't feel like backtracking; I recommend trying it, because it's up-hill until the point of return, with extraordinary beauty in certain spots. It will also give you a lovely view of both Beau Vallon and Bel Ombre, that you won't get anywhere else.

Done? Ok, let's go back to St. Louis road and start descending. Nice curvy road downhill for about 1 Km. At some point you'll find the Beau Vallon Police Station in the middle of an intersection – you'll understand when you get there; go right to Bel Ombre, it's a 3 km straight line where you won't see any sea but instead a very beautiful Church on the left after passing the locally famous night club Tequila Boom. On the right, you'll see the entrance of all major resorts Berjaya, Le Méridien Fisherman's Cove, H Resort.

Following straight, you'll turn back at the bus station next to the La Scala restaurant. Or, for the more adventurous with mountain bike, there's some more 700 m of dirt road up the hill to reach a point where the Anse Majeure trail starts, and you'll have to stop – it's a hiking trail and zero chance of cycling there; I've tried, went a few hundreds of meters and had to give up and go back.

Coming back on Bel Ombre road to the Police Station, turn left, then again turn on your left, at a small intersection that will take you to Coral Strand Hotel and a short 300 m pedestrian walkway right in front of Beau Vallon beach, at the whereabouts of The Savoy Resort. This is the place where the Market Labriz is done every Wednesday around sunset time; gets packed with people, barracks selling street food and souvenirs and sometimes you might see a few Seychellois dancing around a big fire. Noisy. Smoky. Fun!

But you're doing this during the day very early, aren't you? What you'll find is a lot of Russians that wake up at sunrise and pack the beach in front of Savoy.

Continue straight passing the Boat House restaurant on the left. This is a place that has a delicious creole buffet at night; don't recommend it for lunch, because it's "a la carte" and usually takes very long to get served, but food is good and not expensive. Close by, the Baobab pizzeria; well, it's not Italian pizza, but sure looks like the best I've tried in Seychelles and it gets really packed. It's a simple place, at the right price, with sandy floor and beach front – great fun. Get there early if you don't want to spend one hour waiting for table.

The road ahead is scenic and will take you to Glacis, Vista do Mar and Machabee, with the Indian Ocean always on your left side along North Coast road. Beautiful ride and don't think it will be zero altimetry because it will actually be a succession of small hills; your legs will feel it.

North East Point

The beach on Machabee after Carana Beach is noteworthy: a straight line just at the end of a fun 500 m downhill. Pay attention to your speed and go slowly when coming down; there might be some sand banks in the road coasting the sea, which could be tricky. On the right side of the road there is a succession of mini markets fortunately open even at odd times, to replenish your liquids, food, whatever you might need.

At a certain point, with SACOS properties on the left, you'll see a narrow road going up the hill, right after a sharp curve. Pay attention to the cars behind you and plug in a gear to climb.

This is the La Gogue Road, taking you through 3 km of residential houses, to finally reach the dam atop the hill. It's the North part of the island water's reservoir and as far as I know, the only open water reservoir in the country.

The gate is open on the sides, allowing you to go in and explore. It's not allowed to swim and fish. But then with the wealth of the turquoise seas packed with fish right down at the seashore, why would you?

La Gogue Dam

While staring at the dam, you might notice a road going further up-hill. It's just a bit steep but if you take it, you'll go back to Glacis, literally crossing the north tip of Mahé from East to West.

If not, go back 100 m and take the road on the right, descending Maldive Road and you'll end down in La Retraite, basically only 200 m distant from the point where you took the La Gogue Dam road upwards. It's a great detour if you are in for some nice classic climbing!

From La Retraite, you are just 10 minutes away from Victoria. Passing English River, there is a roundabout at the entrance of the city, turn left to Perseverance Island and go explore the new buildings of Forum of Justice and National Assemblée; further, there's the neighborhood of Perseverance, a social housing project that looks very nice indeed, with houses all alike in the Seychelles style of construction, lots of children and a basic organization like Police Station and Local administration.

Going back on the same road, to the main avenue now larger with two lanes in each direction, heading towards Victoria, you'll be almost at the end of this quick tour around North part of Mahé.

Take the Independence Road at the roundabout; pass the Air Seychelles office on the left side, the Museum of National History and its cement crocodile and whale on the right side, and you'll be back at the Clock tower. Just continue straight another 200 m through State House Avenue.

By now you have completed 43.4 km and a total climb of 808 m. Not bad, and we could agree be time for a reward: there's an ice cream coffee shop called "La Dolce Vita" owned by a nice Italian chap. They're equipped with a very "cyclist" Illy Caffè espresso coffee. Dismount and savor!

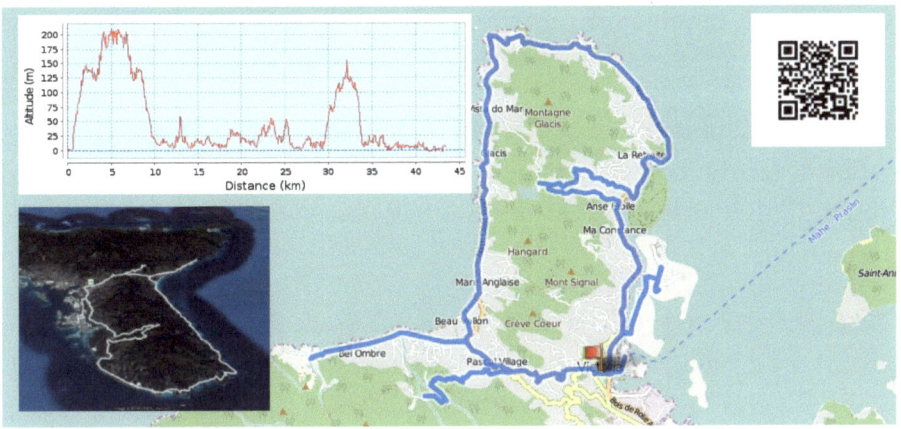

Victoria Override – Currio Road

Victoria is the smallest capital in the whole world. Basically just a few blocks long, with a handful of State buildings well organized around beautiful and organized avenues, and that's it.

Traffic..? Seldom. Or at least, if you're not going around in rush hour, which on this fantastic place in the middle of the Indian Ocean, happens to be religiously every day from about 7 am to 8 am and then again from 4 pm to 5 pm.

If you are driving around town in this narrow time window of rush hour, well... that's a problem because it gets really jammed. Even if you are piloting a bike, it will be a pain to cross the city from one point to the other.

If you are heading to Beau Vallon, a shortcut exists and will be quite handy. On your bike, it represents some climbing which will reward you with some scenic views over Victoria.

 At the first roundabout when you enter city coming from South, turn left, like if you were going on the Old Road back to the airport. About 100 m on the right side of the road, up you go through Liberation Avenue, climbing quickly to 80 m above sea level in less than 200 m, coasting the mountain to discover whole Victoria at your feet on the right.

Continue climbing, merge into Bel Air Road and continue climbing. After a narrow curve, exit the main road into onto Currio Road and you'll find yourself inside a nice neighborhood incrusted into the mountain.

Nice views, a steep and sharp hairpin and back down to interface with Chemin Le Niol. That's it, this route takes you to the top of the St. Louis Road, a few minutes downhill away from Beau Vallon, overriding all of Victoria's transit.

Ports, Reclaimed and Warehouses

I wouldn't say it's an awesome place to go about and roam, but it's the picturesque part of the tour and if you feel like wandering, go here: at the roundabout of Independence Avenue, turn to the direction of Inter-Island Quai; no big deal, you'll end up at the port for the jetty to Praslin & La Digue; there's a nice Oriental restaurant Fish Tail located right next to the quai - not expensive and with quite an impressive option of Oriental dishes, mainly Chinese.

Back again, take left to see the IOT - Indian Ocean Tuna Industries factory; it's the only Tuna preparation factory in Seychelles, and the produce is sold worldwide, at brands like *Pina Gialla* in Italy, for example. It's also the place of Oceania Fisheries, good place to buy fresh and frozen fish at good price and quality.

Back to the roundabout, take the 5th Avenue road, pass in front of the Seychelles Yacht Club, and turn left on Jardin des Enfants to Docklands, interesting vertical shopping with a ramp design and no stairs, climbing up to the 4th floor.

The road goes into the back of Docklands, through the Industrial district, the Seypec (Seychelles Petroleum Company) warehouses, the recently inaugurated STC Hipermarket and that's all folks.

3.2. South East

South East Mahé

We will start our ride at the Eden Island roundabout and take the highway South. The 2 lane fast road starts at the Providence roundabout and goes almost straight and flat until the International Airport of Seychelles. Continuing south and paying attention to traffic between the Airport and Anse Royale, the road will accompany the sea line and be narrow at certain points. This part of the island is heavily populated and this route is best done early morning and weekends, when traffic is lighter.

Anse Aux Pins is a lovely beach with a coral bank almost 2 km long, followed by a small hill that drops you onto Anse Royale, the Fairy Tale beach - one of the most interesting and photogenic beaches in Seychelles. Take the chance of a photo on the left right of the road, there's a parking space and its perfect scenery will have the Fairy Island in the background.

Anse Royale is the most urbanized place in the Southern Mahé. It has a Hospital, some restaurants and it's where University of Seychelles is located. After you pass the small urban center, there's a Church on the left. A cross coming out of the waters, hanging up on a sunken rock makes it the most beautiful site.

Anse Royal

This is the point where the whole shebang changes: traffic ends or at least reduces drastically; the road is gorgeous, still cruising southbound a very beautiful coast. Surfers Beach is the restaurant and guest house on the beach, quick tip is to have lunch there on your way back.

Proceed until the moment the road turns left and you'll go up the Quatre Bornes for around 400 m to the Police Station. Pedal downhill for another 1 km and you'll finally be in the calm, peaceful West Side of Mahé at Takamaka Beach, where the seas are a little bit rougher some times of the year; you will see Takamaka trees lying on the long beach, with sand being blown over the road- requiring some special attention mainly if you are riding a road bike with thin tires.

This 25 km route is a great ride around the South; especially the part after Anse Royal. Not terrific climb, as it's mostly flat, yet still ranging 322 m accumulate ascent; perfect route if combined with the full West Side and eventually going back to Anse Royal, or just climb La Misère or Sans Souci to cross the Island, and this you'll see further ahead when we cover the Climbs.

Old Road

An interesting option to the Highway is the Old Road, starting in Victoria and going southbound, merging back to the main road once you get to the airport. It's a fun lane going through the neighborhoods of Mont Fleuri and Cascade, and not flat at all as you could think by considering that it's almost parallel to the highway: some small hills will account for some more altimetry for your ride. Avoid at night, there's barely any public lightning, and being a densely inhabited road, you will find about everything, from people walking in the dark and in the middle of the road, some dogs that bark and chase you, other ones that will not bark but will just try to grab a byte of you by surprise in the dark. Changing a flat tire at night and in the dark over there is quite difficult.

Police Bay Road; Anse Bazarca and Anse Intendence

Nice 8 km extension when atop the Quatre Bornes hill: turning on the left and going down the sinuous Intendance Road and the charming Grand Police Bay Road for 4 km until you reach Anse Bazarca. It's a beach that is very similar to Anse Takamaka, with difficult seas and currents during part of the year, there are even big red signs alerting not to swim from June to September.

Anse Bazarca

With Takamaka trees leaning over the beach, crystal white sands, blue sea and... Big waves; going back to Quatre Bornes is uphill, steady climbing with good asphalt. At a certain point along the way there's the entrance to the Banyan Tree Resort, which is the same as the public entrance to Anse Intendance: this is another stunning beach, this time with a long sandy strip and big waves for surfers.

3.3. West

We start were we have left turning northwards at the South tip of Mahé, at Anse Takamaka, with its splendid trees of the same name, lying over the unquiet open ocean and the short strip of white sand inviting for a stroll foot naked.

But then, we are not here to dawdle around white sandy beaches almost naked in tropical swimming suits, are we?

Cyclists wear Lycra fabric in shape of bib shorts and jerseys, decorated with flashy helmets and gloves, and we think about riding our bikes all the time, every time, isn't that right? So let's get started going North!

Almost 23 km separate Takamaka from Port Launay, along definitely one of the most beautiful seashores in the world. Very little car traffic, a few neighborhoods concealed amongst the vegetation and on the left, a amazing scenario of marbled blue seas intertwined with all shades of green, luxurious vegetation and big granite boulders, a paradise to ride up and down under the sun and good weather.

The first little village along the way is Baie Lazare. A quick and small climb will introduce you to a Petrol Station and a few local art craft shops. On the left of the road, the beautiful Baie Lazare Catholic Church made of strong brick and stone, always good fresh spiritual repair for the hot sun and high temperatures; on the right, the access to the Kempinsky and Four Seasons' Resort, the same narrow way that is to follow to Anse Soleil, a small secluded beach facing the open ocean with a nice restaurant by the side.

Kids at Baie Lazare

Anse La Mouche follows, and it seems a never-ending succession of beautiful coves. After every curve in the road, a new strip of sand, takamaka trees, little fisherman's boats anchored floating in the waves and the way stretching way ahead along the coast line.

Anse Boileau and Grande Anse, separated by a 2 km easy hill, complete the contour of the shape of West side of Mahé, and you will reach the crossroads to Port Glaude and La Misère right after passing the Avani Barbarons Hotel and three rather strangely shaped electrical towers stranding in front of the Ocean.

At this point, the Grande Anse Petrol Station, with its convenience store, is the ideal place to replenish liquids and food. There's an ATM machine, if you're out of... liquidity!

Anse La Mouche

The beach of Grande Anse is actually 500 m further, close to the Grande Anse Primary School, and it's a long but rather narrow strip of brilliant white sand, rough waves and troubled sea, where again it's forbidden to swim between the months of June to September. Signs all over the extension of the beach mark the danger. Just resist the calling of the mermaids and continue riding!

Cyclists love challenges by nature, and this "walk in the park" along the West coast couldn't come without a hurdle: the highest altitude of the coastline on the West side of the Island, is a 2.5 km long steep hill, starting at the beginning of the Grande Anse Village, where there has been now inaugurated an STC supermarket, and climbs up-hill for a good 5 minutes under the sun.

Port Glaude is at the end of the descent, marked by the Primary School and the bifurcation up to Sans Souci and the East side, just 15 km away. It's worthwhile to ride further north for some 3 km more, passing the Del Place restaurant, the access road to Constance Ephelia, enjoying the mangroves along the way, to reach Port Launay, probably a pirate's cove, marked by emerald colored seas and big corals that can be seen from the shores.

A wooden cross planted on top of a grey boulder in the middle of the sea gives the place a charming setup, only barely disturbed by the customers of the Resort, immerse in several under-water activities.

Port Launay

3.4. The Climbs

In Mahé there are only 2 big overpasses from one side of the Island to the other, that reach altitude above 400 m: Sans Souci Road and La

Misère Road. These are the two champions, title-holders in matter of altitude and are great fun for all the climbing-loving cyclists. Prepare for at least 1h up-hill each side, of each one of them.

Other alternatives are Montagne Posée, Les Canneles and Quatre Bornes: shorter and with less accumulated climbing. Montagne Posée is steep and sinuous from both ways, fairly challenging if you take it fast thinking it will be easy, you might find yourself half way up with no breath at all. Les Canneles is lighter and shorter. Quatre Bornes instead, with a constant slope, is the Southernmost route crossing from one side of the Island to the other, and it's is rather quick and easy, reason for which just this specific one will not be covered separately but within other bigger rides.

Going Up Sans Souci from West to East

Sans Souci Road

This is my absolute favorite side-to-side overpass: categorically scenic! Going East-West, it intertwines a steep 9 Km up to the highest point (483 m), with a series of small hills atop the mountain for about 2 km, and then straight downhill through a series of narrow and angled hairpins to reach Port Glaude by the sea. Paradise!

Along the way, there are a couple of highlights.

The first one of these is the "Mission Lodge". According to the Seychelles Heritage Foundation, this place was originally called Venn's Town, where Missionaries ran a school for slaves that have been liberated after 1861.

The only thing left from these times is the ruins of the buildings, found along the property, and the gazebo where Queen Elizabeth II, in Her Majesties' one and only official visit to the country once sat to have tea in 1972, overlooking the horizon. Located in the succession of small hills atop Sans Souci Road, right before starting the descent to the Tea Factory, is accessible through a narrow paved road that goes slightly up to a parking place.

The bike can be carried on your shoulder to the viewpoint which is perhaps the most famous vantage point in all Seychelles, with a spectacular view spanning great part of the West side of the Island looking south, and offering an unforgiving sight of the carefully cut and designed geography of beaches, hills, mountains and sea. Surely deserves a visit!

The second highlight is the "Tea Factory", just 200 meters after you start descending Sans Souci Road to reach Port Glad. We can see it coming by the plantations of tea trees by the side of the road when you are approaching the main entrance of the place. Established in 1962, in the cool mountain air of Morne Blanc, it's the only facility for growing and manufacturing tea in the country. Features splendid panoramic views, and a small coffee-shop (or should I say tea-shop) and there is the possibility of taking guided tours around the tea plantations terrace over terrace. The commercial part has not been ignored: you can buy their favorite tea flavors to take back home.

As a remark, along Sans Souci road one can find the access points for two of the most famous hiking trails: Copolia trail, up to 497 m high, and a breathtaking view of East side over St. Anne Marine Park; best of all, just within reach of 1 hour moderately easy hiking. That will be at Km 5.7, on the left side of the road after passing the Copolia Lodge.

The other one is the trail to access Morne Blanc Mountain, which is 675 m high, very close to the highest point in Mahé: Morne Seychellois ranging 905 m tall. As mentioned, its access is rather close to the Tea Factory, at approximately 10 km from the start of the Sans Souci Road.

Total 14.21 km; Total Climb: 605 m; Riding Westbound: 7 km climbing, 3 km in the hilly plateau, 4.1 km descending; steeper if riding Eastbound.

La Misère Road

It's just plain steep unforgiving climbing all the way up, taking you to 439 m, almost as high as Sans Souci tops, and then downhill to the other side of the Island. It will push hard on your lungs and legs; anyway you take it, as the inclination of the climbing on one side is practically the same as the descent on the other.

La Misère Viewpoint

Take it Westbound and you'll reach the La Misère viewpoint on km 1.8 offering a chance to catch your breath and awarding you a stunning view of capital Victoria and its neighborhoods: from Mont Fleuri on the North, to Eden Island and the spectacular flock of islands that make up St. Anne Marine Park, then Cascade way South and peeking over the airport at the edge of the frame.

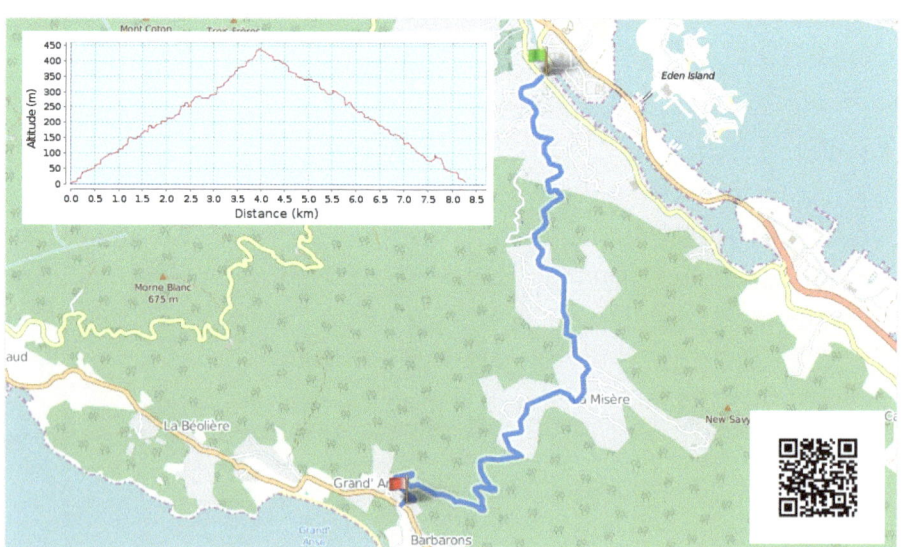

Montagne Posée

Every time I take Montagne Posée Road, I start off very confident, sprint a little at the entry point to release the tension on the legs and then start going up, at a buoyant fast pace.

It's a 5.7 km stretch between Anse Boileau on the West Side and Anse aux Pins on the East, and it's a good option if you are about the airport or close by boroughs and want to enjoy some quiet calm time in the bucolic West, without having to go through La Misère.

Inevitably, after a few curves the inclination rises and it gets serious. Comes to the extent of wishing the peak is right after the next curve – and it's never there- and also regretting all that wasted energy sprinting at the very beginning.

What I mean to say, this is a tricky sinuous climb, great fun up to Bon Espoir at 248 m in just little less than 3 km. It's steep both ways, so you get to double the fun by doubling the opportunities to do different routes.

Who would have said that Seychelles is all about climbing?

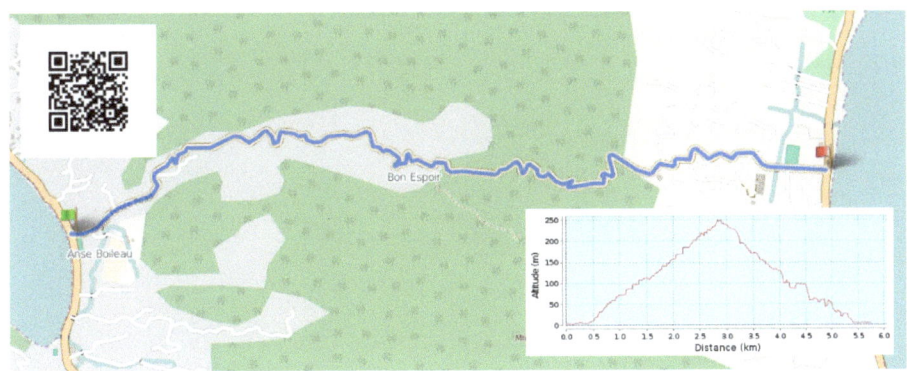

Les Canelles Road and Back-Road

This one is a smoother 1.5 km climb and the same distance descent, starting off at Anse Royale, at the intersection with the Church, and ending up on the other side in Anse La Mouche.

A variation of Les Canelles road to make it exciting, is taking the back road up the hill passing over next to the Canelles peak. Serious climbing up to 222 m in just 2.5 km: you'll find a few lower gears might be missing in your bike.

If you're looking for a good treat to your climber's badge, take both roads in a 10 km circular ride, starting and ending at Anse Royale, the road first, then coming back through the back. Serious business!

4. The Big Rides

All the pieces and bits of cycling pleasure and scenic landscape seen before, come together in longer rides up to 60 km, ideally starting very early in the morning to avoid the mounting temperature and rock-solid sunlight, especially if combined with one or a few climbs East-West and vice-versa, which might become progressively challenging when approaching mid-day.

4.1. The North Loop

Doing North loop is a "quick and dirty" 21 km with a little bit more than 300 m of amassed climb, mainly along the succession of small hills alongside the road. Fast workout or just a ride to clear out your mind, it's great for the scenery along the shoreline, and just St Louis Road at the end of it, to mash some substance, terminate the ride in sleek style, and to be worth the sausages and eggs you got for breakfast!

Machabee

Typical predictable starting point: the Clock Tower monument in Victoria. Favorite place for after-ride decompression espresso: La Dolce Vita. Can't help it!

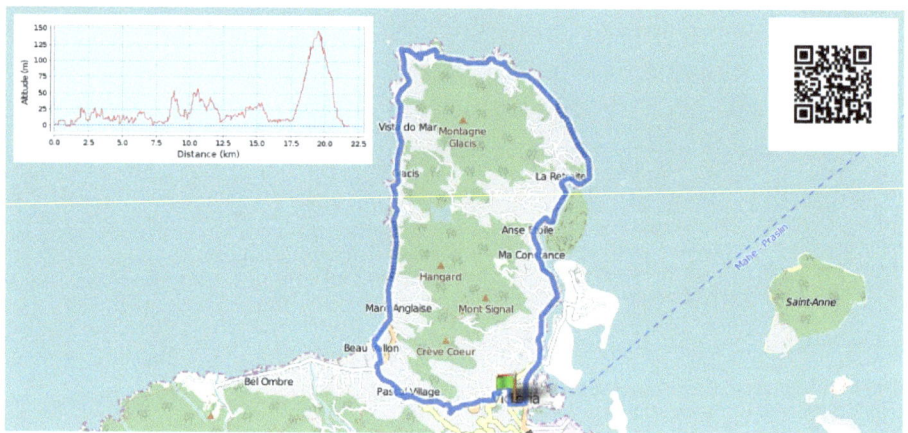

4.2. The Two Peaks Ride

I've called this ride "Two peaks" but looking at the altimetry you can see straight out there's actually a third, midget peak in the middle.

Ride up Sans Souci to the hilly plateau, quite close to Morne Blanc peak. Patch down on West side to find the 2.5 km long little "midget" peak, and left at the Grande Anse petrol station to La Misère.

It's a total of 30 Km, of which only 4 km on flats – less than 15% of the distance. All the rest is either up or down, and steep as steep can get, for a total climb of 1.194 m.

Good thing about this ride is that you have two different levels of challenge if you do it clock or counter-clock wise.

Since Sans Souci is steeper West to East, and La Misère is basically the same any ways you take it, the overall steepness is completely different: actually much challenging if you ride it clock-wise!

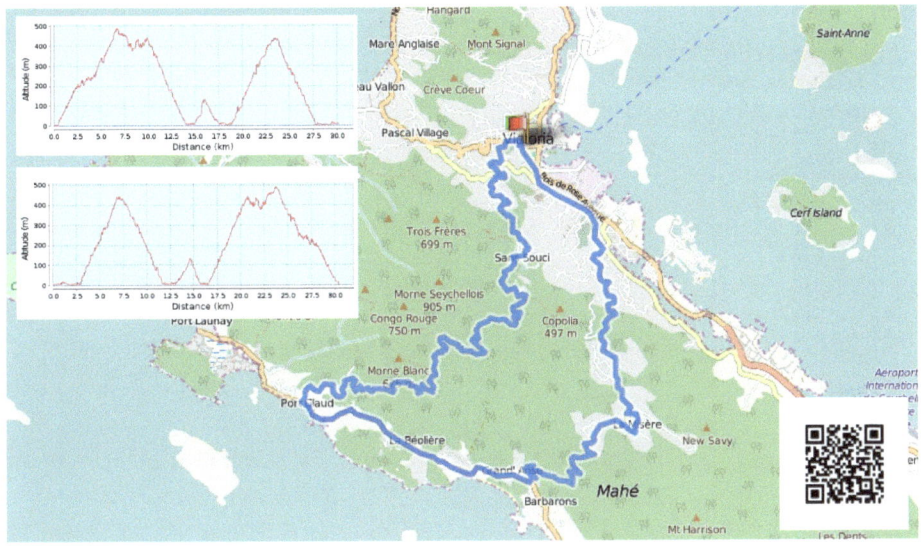

4.3. The South + 1 Peak

There are a couple of options here: you can ride down South and come back taking La Misère West to East, for some merciful 56 km, 1042 m climb, granting a modest successful sense of triumph – especially if you're in a hurry to get back home and enjoy your well-earned massage to sour muscles!

Or, you can extend a little bit more, take the Sans Souci upwards from the East Side –remember, it's the steeper direction!- and finalize with true sense of accomplishment following some heavy-duty 64 km, 1360m.

Doesn't seem much more than the other, but wait until you arrive in Port Glaude after a couple of hours on the saddle and hammering strong on the pedals, and you see the hill-top just waiting to be scaled in front of you. Punk!

Either way, it's a fantastic journey out and amongst my favorites and more often ridden!

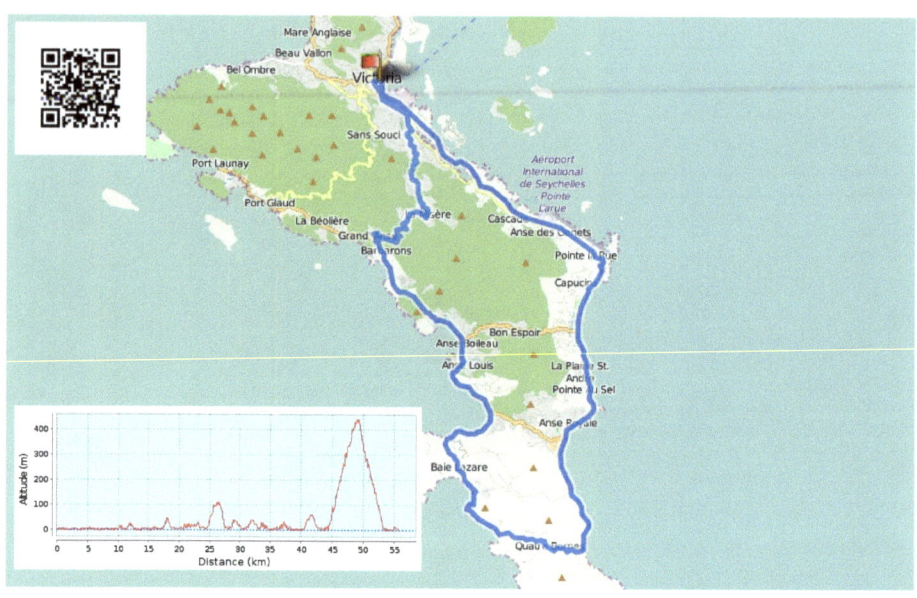

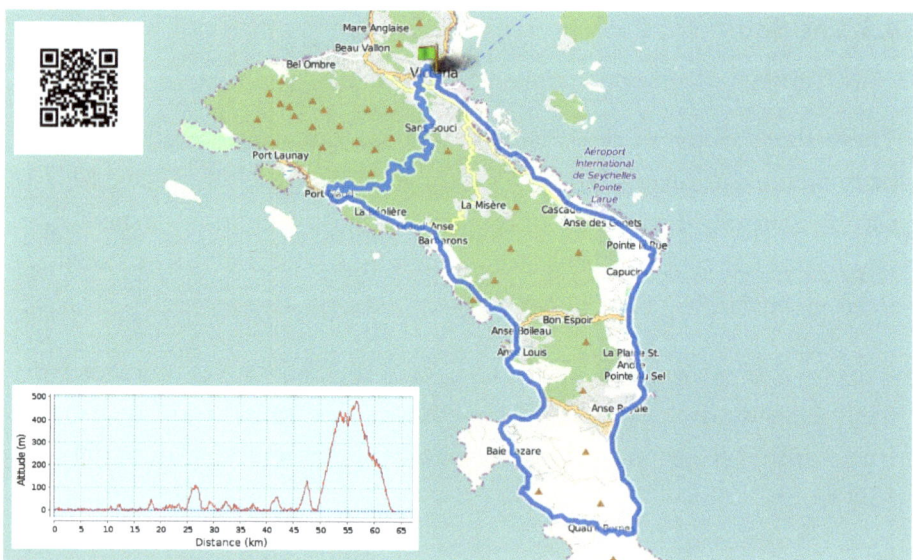

5. The Really Big Rides

Achieving longer rides in Seychelles represent quite a challenge: due to the geography, long distances without repetition the same roads are hard to find and to combine, and always come associated to strong altimetry - for a rider to cycle 80 km in Seychelles, will need at least 5 hours of good pace and strong measure of resistance because of the heat, humidity, wind and sunlight.

If you're used to do the typical 130+ km on flat km-crunching roads, you'll see that in Seychelles that will more or less equate in effort, time and calories to the 80+ km.

So, if you're embarking into this kind of challenge, you'll need to wake up and get out there riding very early, hydrate often, ensure you eat at periodical intervals to keep the energy and stamina at decent levels, and then just ride and take advantage of the magnificent landscape.

I've made sure you would find next to each one of these longer rides description, the QR code in www.gpsies.com where you can not only view the course but also download it to your preferred GPS device.

Very important to take note is that, as with any long rides and not only in Seychelles, if you can, team up to make the ride more fun, a collective effort and to have someone to talk to along the route. Riding with other people also motivates you to wake up early – no one wants to disappoint friends that are waiting for you, right?!

Establish a nice target as point of arrival, maybe a place where you can have a coffee, a cold beer, or just fresh water to celebrate the moment, and here you go!

5.1. Tour of the Island, ending at "The Boardwalk"

The Tour is a full loop, starting at the Eden Island round-about, moving directly South taking the Providence Highway to the International Airport. A variation of this could be taking the old road if you're not in the mood for the two fast lane's highway traffic route.

From the airport, straight South again along Pointe La Rue, Anse Au Cap until Anse Royal; this part of the route has sometimes heavy traffic, so it's good to do it early in the morning and same traffic is the reason why it's better to start the Tour going South instead of North, to avoid riding Anse Royal around noon, when it seems everybody is on their wheels. But then again, strong traffic in Seychelles is quite relative and it's not an impeditive!

At Anse Royal, there's place to replenish liquids in several small shops in the small village center in case you haven't yet done so.

Continuing South, and as already mentioned before, the moment you pass the Catholic Church of Anse Royal, you will notice a complete different change of pace: there's almost no traffic at all, you see just a few constructions along the road and the get-aways to the Southern back-roads, until you reach the Surfers Point, at Anse Forbans neighborhood, before going West and up Quatre Bornes.

Continuing from the Southwest tip of Mahé at Anse Takamaka, up the coast until Port Glaude, it will take you 1-2 hours depending on your pace. Pit stop to replenish at the Grand Anse Petrol Station, as you'll still be half-way the Tour and some tough climb ahead.

You can take a decision here, of just taking La Misére up, shortening the ride by 10 km, or continue as planned, further north-west and then climb by Sans Souci. Assess your willingness to continue, the temperature, humidity, glycogen fuel cells and just go.

Continuing up Sans Souci for an 8 Km climb, reaching an altitude of 486 meters above sea level, with stretches up to 14% inclination, you will pass the Tea Factory and cross the Island to Victoria. Go down Bel Air Road until you reach Revolution Avenue, close to The Barrel and the Police Station, and then up to climb the hill to Beau Vallon.

Alternatively, you can take the Victoria override (Currio Road) to avoid traffic but will shorten your Tour by 3 km and scratch some altimetry as well – you don't want to do that, do you?

Continuing through Beau Vallon, you will reach the Island North tip and then turn East to complete the loop back to Victoria, already just a few km distant from your goal.

At Eden Island, park around "The Boardwalk", sit down and replenish carbohydrates enjoying a local Seybrew, to wipe the dust away from your throat.

With the big super-yachts in the background at Eden Marina, clean that ugly salty grin out of your face and pretend you can still smile after 4 hours, 84 km and 1750 m of climbs. From there you can just pick one of the dozens of splendid beaches in the Island to unwind and spend the rest of the day with your family. Mission accomplished.

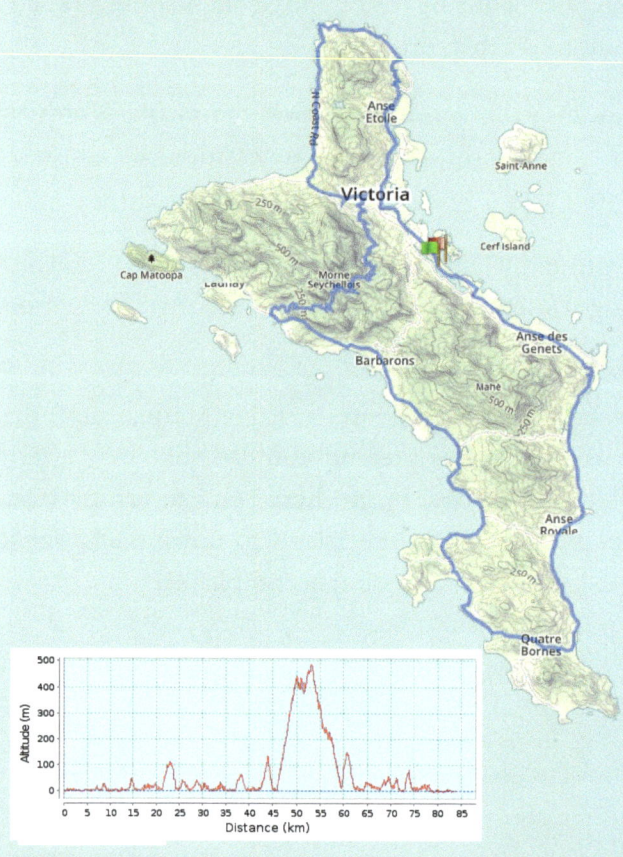

83.77 km (round trip)
Total climb: 1750 m, Total descent: 1750 m
Altitude range 489 m (Altitude from: -3 m to 486 m)

© CAntunes | © Mapbox | © OpenStreetMap contributors | iText 4.2.0 | ID: lhzpwhlwdcvjqlil

5.2. Shoreline, ending with the traditional *espresso* at "La Dolce Vita"

The Shore Line is a back-and-forth very long 128 km ride starting and ending in Victoria at the cafeteria "La Dolce Vita", without any strong peak but fairly high altimetry (2.056 m climbing) spread out along the way in several small hills. There will be no serious climbs, no overpasses, just riding (almost) flat all the way and back through same route. If you're riding in a group, La Dolce Vita is a good meeting spot, as there's plenty of parking place if you're coming by car.

Clock Tower in Victoria

We start climbing St. Louis Road to Beau Vallon, go through the Savoy cycling promenade, passing in front of La Plage restaurant to find yourself back on North Coast road. Full throttle North and straight back into Victoria, then South, heading to the Airport via the Old Road, reaching Anse Royal and up the hill Quatre Bornes to touch Anse Takamaka.

West Coast will then take you North all the way until you reach Port Launay. You can stretch 4 km more by going through a narrow paved road until Baie Ternay, a beautiful -and most of the times- deserted and secluded beach.

Turnaround and moving south you'll pass the gateway to Constance Ephilia, along beautiful mangroves, then the beautiful Anse L'Islet with the small island that refers to its name engrained in front of Del Place restaurant.

L'Islet

Don't forget to replenish liquids and food at the Petrol Station in Grand Anse, as you'll be counting 65 km already and still at roughly half the way, needing 2-3 more hours to finish the challenge.

South passing the 3 big electrical towers on the right you'll see the Avani Barbarons Resort, and continuing through Anse Boileu, Baie Lazare and the very bucolic roads of the South, where the sea is stronger and bluer and you almost don't see anyone around.

After 100 km, the climb from Takamaka to Quatre Bornes will in fact seem tough but as promised, it's actually one of the few places where you'll have to use your lower gears in this long route.

On the last 25 km to Victoria you will expect some traffic but no major worries, just ride with caution and be visible.

Returning to La Dolce Vita after more than 4-5 hours and almost 130 km in your knees sure call for a coffee; the friendly Italian owner of the place will for sure welcome you and your friends to celebrate the tough ride with an "espresso".

There is a shorter variation of this route: just cutting out the 20 km of North loop and it will take it down to 108 km and 1645 climbing. But you don't want to dare cutting short of the challenge, do you?

Ahhhh.... Espresso!

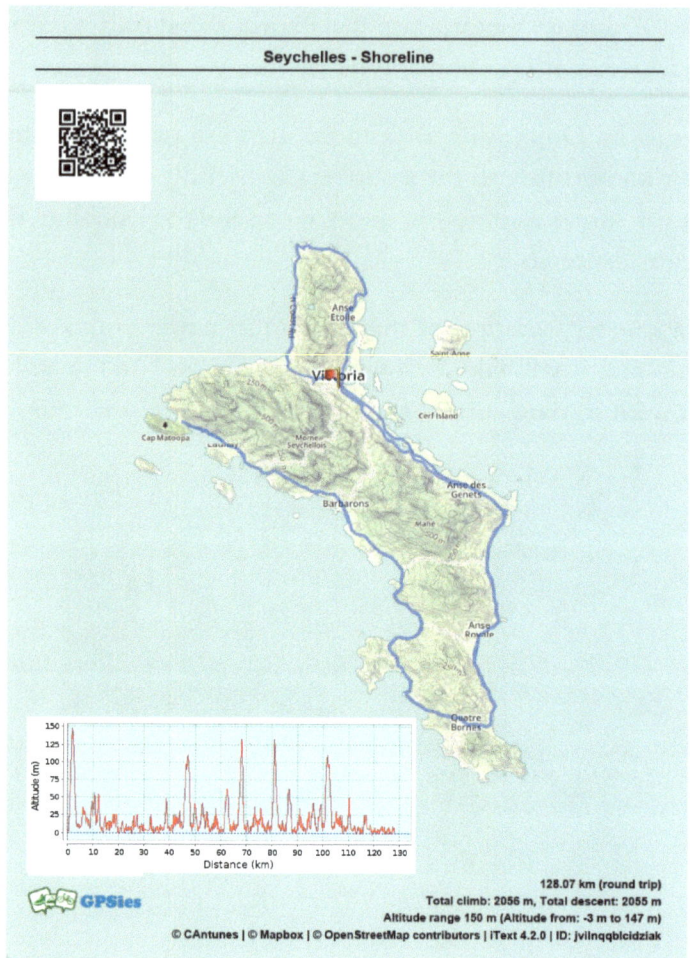

128.07 km (round trip)
Total climb: 2055 m, Total descent: 2055 m
Altitude range 150 m (Altitude from: -3 m to 147 m)
© CAntunes | © Mapbox | © OpenStreetMap contributors | iText 4.2.0 | ID: jvilnqqblcidziak

GPSies

5.3. "Cyclist Middle East" Tour of the Island, ending in Victoria

A quick background on this one: around May 2016 I had the idea to contact the editor of the cycling magazine "Cyclist Middle East" published in Abu Dhabi by Motivate Publishing, to bluntly invite a team of a reporter and a photographer to visit the Island and make Seychelles the cover story for the magazine. What better place, just little more than 4 hours away from any country in GCC, well connected by air to Abu Dhabi, with big hills, steep climbs, dense forests, scenic views, cinematographic landscape, well cared curvy roads, great weather, for a cyclist to trade the sand of the desert by the sand of the beaches?

Andy, the editor of the Magazine, immediately accepted my invitation to come himself in July, peak of Summer in Abu Dhabi reaching sometimes above 45 degrees, to find the best temperature of the year, just around 28 degrees in Mahé - the deal would be that I would go around and show them the best of the best of Mahé. Andy asked me "Can we ride Saturday and Sunday", and I just replied "Yeah mate – of course, let's do it!" – Cyclist mentality!

We just put together a mix of Tour of the Island with a loop at the South and the two steepest hills Sans Souci and La Miseré in the same route, and went around on a Saturday morning, for about 8 hours, followed by a pick-up with John our photographer. Life is hard on a saddle, if you're trying to get the best photos.

I can't tell you how many times we went up and down on one of the hairpins of St. Louis Road... either we were too fast, then too slow, or a car got in the middle, we must have done that at least 10 times. The same thing in several other spots of the island, and it was great fun!

The itinerary rendezvoused at the Clock Tower in Victoria. The spot! From there we went up the beautiful coast to Machabee, followed by Vista del Mar already facing Silhouette Island, and finally Beau Vallon.

From there, we took St. Louis Road heading Victoria and when in town, we went straight up through Bel Air to take Sans Souci Road.

Fifteen km later, in Port Glaude on the other side of the Island, we did the little stretch connecting Port Launay along the mangroves to capture one of the most beautiful spots of the whole tour, L'Islette.

From there we u-turned South to Anse Boileau, took Les Canelles up the hills - short but quite steep climb to the East side giving way to Anse Aux Pins. Almost lost my whole energy there!

South again to Anse Royal and Anse Forbans and then uphill again, through Quatre Bornes, the secluded beaches of Takamaka, then Baie Lazare, full North along the coast, and arriving at Barbarons, deep breath with already more than 85 km and 1800 m climb on our legs – up-hill to La Misére and back to Eden Island.

This is a great 96 km ride with 2.380 m climbing. It's the one I absolutely recommend if you want to taste the best ascent and descent with a dosage of long distance.

An additional ride from your home and back, or a tour down to the airport along the old road and back on the highway, will pump your distance to 115 Km or more.

The readers of Cyclist Middle East have had the possibility of reading the article by Andy Sherwood and photos by John Marsland on their September 2016 issue.

The "Cyclist Middle East" Tour of The Island

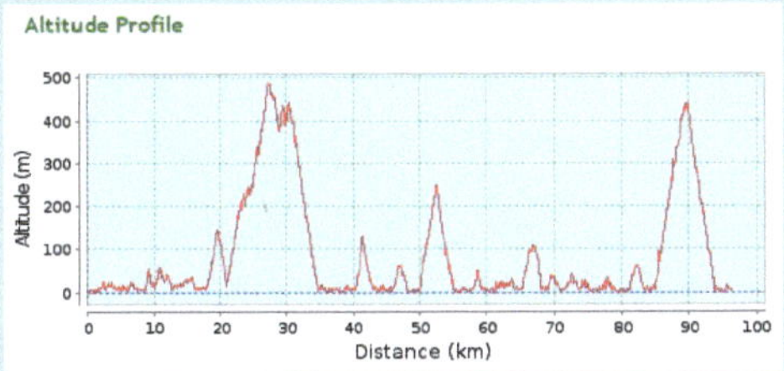

Altitude Profile

96.29 km (round trip)
Total climb: 2380 m, Total descent: 2380 m
Altitude range 488 m (Altitude from: -2 m to 486 m)

GPSies

5.4. Praslin & La Digue

If you're staying in Mahé and want to go for a weekend ride to the other islands or just a one day "back-pack"ride away like I did once, put Praslin and La Digue in the equation and here's your great deal.

Buy your Air Seychelles ticket online and board the quick and comfortable 15 minute flight connecting Mahé to Praslin; the national carrier operates more than 25 domestic round-trip flights a day between the two main islands and will take your bike within your normal baggage allowance; like any other airline, someone will ask you to empty the pressure of your bike tires, and take off your wheels – a bit of a annoyance, especially the part of emptying your tires, considering you won't fly pressurized, but safety first. Prepare to pump them up upon arrival.

Don't forget to pay close attention to the derailleur hanger when you take the rear wheel off; if you break that (which might happen more often than not) you're done! Have I mentioned that there's no bike store on the country? And that if you need a replacement part in Seychelles, most probably you'll have to go online and will take some time to arrive? Idle time off-bike, try kayaking...!

Airport Domestic Terminal – checking-in the bike

Now, the must see places are "Vallée de Mai" and "Anse Lazio". Vallée de Mai is a Unesco World Heritage Site and said to be the original "Garden of Eden". Anse Lazio is "just" one of the most beautiful beaches in the world...

The Twin-Otter aircraft upon arrival in Praslin; just 15 minutes away!

Praslin

Praslin is the second largest Island of the archipelago, with a population of over 8.000 people. 35 km long and just 7 km wide, it is quite smaller in comparison to Mahé – if you could think of that!

To get to Vallée de Mai, go Eastbound along the coast until a bifurcation on the left, then there's a 3 km climb to get there.

Pralin's Southern Shores

I recommend you take advantage of the beautiful shoreline of this part of Praslin, take right instead and you will follow along the coast until you reach the Jetty, then Baie St. Anne and only then left uphill to Vallée de Mai. This extension will add almost 10 km to your ride. The road is gorgeous, in the middle of luxurious vegetation.

When you start getting closer to the Vallée de Mai Nature Reserve, you begin to advert a glimpse of the exuberant endemic nature: the most famous of which the giant palm trees –whose leaves can achieve more than 18 kg each- bearing the famous world's biggest seed "Coco de Mer" (called like that because they were usually find afloat in the Ocean and the sailors thought they would come from underwater forests). Vallée de Mai is the only place in the world where the "Lodoicea Maldivica" grows and produces its seeds in nature, with the typical shape of... a women's butt.

Some other endemic species of "moving"palm trees with multiple roots growing outside the soil, and spines prevent the giant Aldabra Turtles of eating their branches, are found in Praslin and mainly in Vallée de Mai. The world's smallest frog is also an illustrious inhabitant of the National Park, as well as a black big geko lizard that lives on the giant palm trees.

Arriving in Vallée de Mai, there's plenty of parking space and a few bike stands on the other side of the road where to hook up your bike. The staff will not allow you to park your bike closer to the main building, or attach it with a locker anywhere, but it's all pretty safe. Entrance is free for local residents.

The visit will take you 1 to 2 hours, and I do recommend you take a guide to help you locate and understand the amazing diversity of the "Garden of Eden".

You will want to ride on the plain brilliant white thin sands of Cote D'Or beach, almost 2 km long – if you are riding a mountain bike, of course. There are a few access points to the beach. I was told you can't ride your bike on the beaches in Seychelles, but I actually don't know if that really applies, I personally never had any problem. Go slowly, anyway.

From there to Anse Lazio, once considered by Lonely Plate the most beautiful beach in Praslin and one of the best in the archipelago, is just little bit more than 6 km along the beautiful coast of Anse Possession and Anse Takamaka.

Along the road you will notice the Raffles Resort: right at the beginning when you see the indication, there's a shortcut on the right that takes pedestrians and cyclists through the Resort, to come out the other way on the same road.

This will avoid a steep climb of 200 m up the hill and give you a taste of the Resort look & feel – surely the main objective for that shortcut!

Back on the paved road; prepare to climb a steep 300 m long hill that gives access to the beach. From above you will see the Sea and overlook the beautiful extension of Anse Lazio below.

The beach is decorated by large granite boulders and palm trees that lie bedding on the beach sands.

The Bonbom Plume restaurant tucked behind the tree line has an interesting menu with seafood salads, fish options and cold drinks for lunch, at a good cost-benefit. The service is good -which in Seychelles never means fast-, the washrooms are remarkably clean and you will eat your lunch on the sands. There are other options for lunch down the beach.

The 12 km stretch back to the East side of the Island follows the same route, and can be calmly bridged in a little bit more than 1 hour to the port, which is important to notice if you are going to take the interisland jetty to La Digue. These have scheduled departures, which are different depending of day of week.

You can buy the ticket there directly and I suggest you get round-trip, so you are done with it and reserve your place on the return. Clarify to the clerk that you will be carrying a bicycle; it will come at an additional cost. It will take around 15 to 20 minutes to reach La Digue.

Anse Lazio

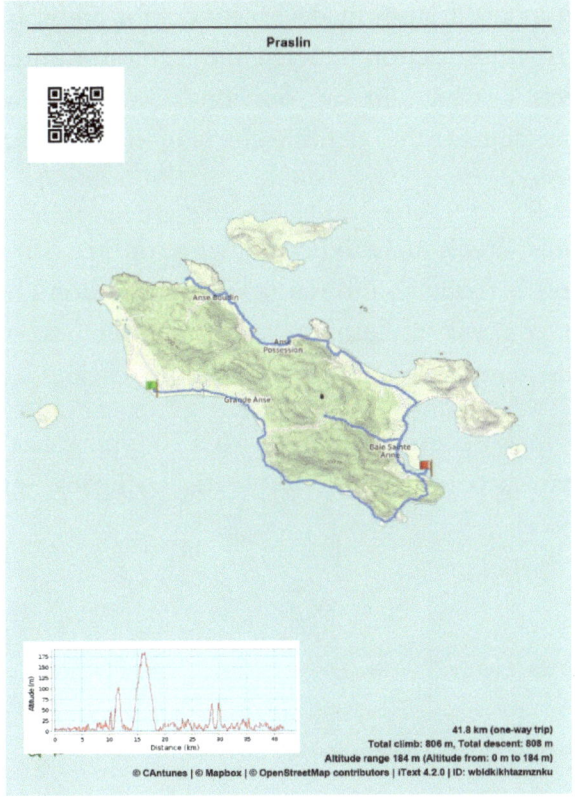

La Digue

The third largest inhabited island of Seychelles is awesome! Planted in a granitic seabed at just 3 km East from Praslin and discovered by the French Navigator Lazare Picault in 1742, La Digue was first colonized in 1790 and just little more than 2.800 people currently live there.

There is no airport in the island, the access via inter-island jetty is easy and takes only 15 minutes from Praslin. There is also a fast boat service directly from Mahé, running a few times a day, and the crossing takes approximately 1 hour.

Although La Digue is significantly smaller than Praslin, it appears cozier and to have many more interesting places to visit. This is certainly due to the fact that there are almost no motorized means of transportation in the Island, made exception for an ambulance, a few vehicles to carry construction material and just a few others from some exclusive hotels – which in my opinion should review this option somehow to maintain the definitively slow-motion-almost-stopping appeal of the place.

Bikes rule undisputedly here! The moment you get off the jetty, you will have people offering you to rent a bike. If you don't have yours, do it. Otherwise you will go around walking, which would be a pity considering the many places you can see around cycling.

The bikes for rental come equipped with a shopping cart on the back, where you can accommodate you stuff: backpack, groceries, and shopping bags.

Northeast of La Digue

Don't miss the opportunity to check-in into a hotel. Or just stay in a guest house, or even a self-catering establishment: there are plenty there and will allow you to savor the night life (or the absence of it), relaxing outdoors overlooking a fully stared sky without equal in this region of the world.

Take advantage of the day to stroll around and bike up and down. A nice ride along the coast to the North and Northeast side will not be longer than 10 km round trip from the Jetty berth place at La Digue Marina. The scenery is great, you will cross some nice establishments with beach right in front of the paved road, where you can lie down and enjoy the sun.

Last time I was there I was able to see some Giant Tortoises walking around with in proud centenary wise age and more than 200 kg, right in the middle of the road, undisturbed and un-disturbable.

I've also seen a few giant centipedes crossing the road. And when I'm saying giant, I'm talking about the largest insect I've ever seen, at least 30 cm long – silly gigantic!

Following our tour of the Island, the must go place is through the L'Union Estate Farm, with its collection of spices and plants – including a huge plantation of vanilla that spreads the soft and sweet smell of that delicacy around the whole compound.

In the same Farm, on your way to Anse Source D'Argent, there is a precinct with dozens of giant Tortoises, which you can touch and feed with green leaves purposely left on top of a bench.

Be careful, they seem slow and quiet, but they're quite reactive when you are holding their lunch; they don't usually bite but if they do, it's told to be a strong grip!

Giant Tortoises in La Digue

Located at the end of the Farm, restaurant Lanbousier is known for being the best cost-benefit of the Island. Exaggeration or not, it is open from 12:00 to 15:00 every day and with a fixed selection of local dishes and curries and will make the happiness of the sorrow bikers that have been going around the island since early morning.

Just about 200 m ahead, after crossing a little cement bridge, you will open your eyes in disbelief: it will seem to you –at least it seemed to me!- the most beautiful place on the planet! Actually, Anse Source

D'Argent has been distinguished for several times as one of the top 5 beaches in the world.

Its granitic boulders, the crystalline waters, the marine fauna and flora, the coconut trees lying over the sands providing shade in small secluded little bays, separating the "Anses" in several smaller private beaches, make it all absolutely spectacular.

You won't get to pedal there; if you are riding a rental bike, you can leave it in front of Lanbousier. No one will take it from there, you can relax. Don't ask me why and how come, but it's the way things work in La Digue.

Instead if you are using your own bike, to which you are affectionate, well just push it through the sands until you find the perfect spot for your afternoon of "dolce farniente"!

Anse Source D'Argent

The other ride with amazing views —everything around La Digue is an amazing view!- is crossing from the West to the East to Grande Anse, following a narrow paved road that stretches 3 km up the mountain, starting at the left of the gates of L'Union Estate Farm, at a very moderate slope.

It's not quite a climb; it's just an inclination, easy-easy. And on the other side of the Island you'll find a breathtaking scenario of big blue-as-blue-can-get waves and multicolored granitic boulders decorating each of the extremities of the perfectly white sandy beach and a small bar.

Dismount your bike and breathe in. Ask for a really frozen Seybrew – made in Seychelles!

Now... just enjoy Paradise on Earth!

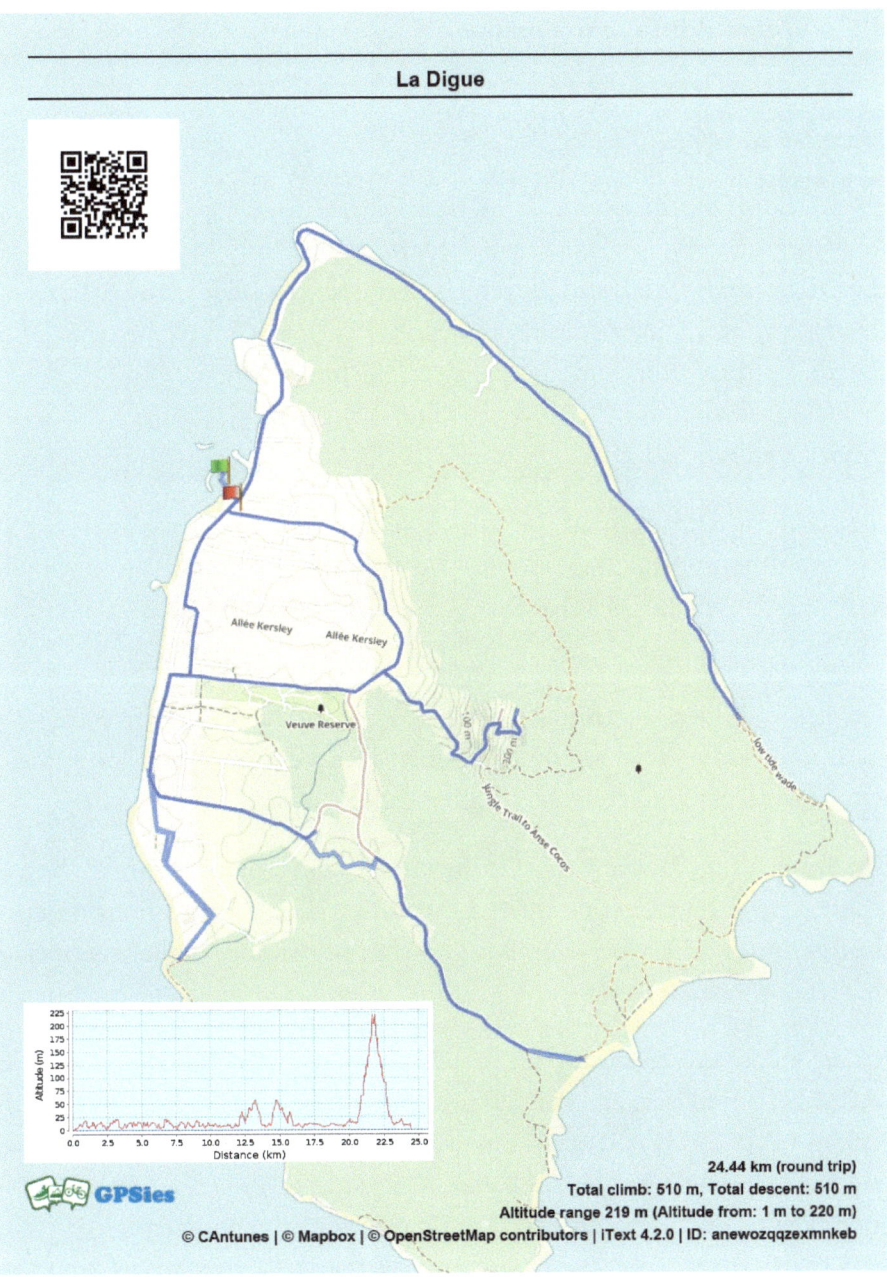

Allée Kersley Allée Kersley

Veuve Reserve

Jungle Trail to Anse Cocos

low tide wade

24.44 km (round trip)
Total climb: 510 m, Total descent: 510 m
Altitude range 219 m (Altitude from: 1 m to 220 m)

GPSies

© CAntunes | © Mapbox | © OpenStreetMap contributors | iText 4.2.0 | ID: anewozqqzexmnkeb

6. Additional info and Thanks

All routes, without exception, have been ridden, several times and personally.

Maps are courtesy of Lucia and Riccardo from Jolly Maps, a company that distributes the best and most complete Guides and Maps of Seychelles, at all major trade shows in Europe. Comprehensive of a foldable pocket map and an app available for iPhone an Android, it is the best reference for "what do to" and "where to stay" that I've found for Seychelles.

All photos are property of the author –taken with a smartphone; except for one riding up-hill Sans Souci, and another in English River, which were taken by John Marsland for Cyclist Middle East issue September 2016.

Thanks to Giuseppe from La Dolce Vita, for having resurrected my spirit and body, so many times after my Saturday morning long rides, with that magic liquid elixir of that he calls *espresso*!

Thanks to The Boardwalk, for being the only place close to home where I have had the possibility of savoring a really cold freezing gut-dust-cleaning beer after a boiling hot day out riding, while overseeing the beautiful marina boats.

Route maps and altimetry are courtesy of www.GPSies.com, a great online mapping service that allows you to upload, create and share cycling routes. Has a remarkably user friendly interface and the best is that it comes for free! If you have a QR code reader, can just scan the code next to the maps, and you'll be directed to the course page.

Thanks to the people of Seychelles, especially the drivers of all kind of vehicles that have gently shared the roads with me.

And thanks to my wife Ana Carolina, once again, for thousand many different reasons but also for having rescued me a few times around the Island, from mechanical failures, flat tires in excess or simply after Human failure, under the scorching sun without energy, water or food anymore.

Thanks to my readers, for taking the time to share the imagination of my stories.

And hope you will enjoy riding your bicycle in Seychelles as much as I did!